CAN THIS WOLF SURVIVE?

RAFAEL ZEPEDA

Angels Flight Books

ISBN: 978-1-7337848-1-8

Angels Flight Books
Published and distributed in the United States by Angels Flight Books.

Director: Kareem Tayyar
Book design by: Karen Mao
www.angelsflightbooks.com

Some of the poems from this collection first appeared in the following publications:

Huizache, Chiron Review, Golden Streetcar, Nerve Cowboy, Swink, and Adventures in the Unknown Interior of My Mind.

For Marcia

TABLE OF CONTENTS

HE HAD TO CATCH A PLANE

He'd been out on the reservation
south of Shiprock
for a week with no shower
and very little water to drink,
just illegal light beer that he didn't much care for.

And the dust of the reservation roads and twisters
was all over his face, neck, armpits,
in his boots and in his mouth
so that every bite of his fry bread and beans
crunched between tiny granules of sand
between his teeth.

His Navajo friend of fifty years, Taylor,
drove his pickup south through the reservation,
then up into the White Mountains and Apache country,
then down toward Globe,
barreling along at eight-five and ninety
toward Phoenix Airport and the plane that he
wanted to take to L. A.

"No problem," Taylor said.
It was an hour-and-fifteen minutes until take off,
then an hour, then forty-five minutes and,
when they pulled up to the door,
thirty minutes until take off,
the plane starting its engines.

He said adios, grabbed his bag
and ran to the desk,

then ran again toward the gate,
his clothes soaked through and through,
his t-shirt sticking to him,
the sweatband on his cowboy hat as wet as rain,
dust grinding his skin under his shirt and Levi's.

At the gate, he fumbled out his ticket,
then went into the plane full-to-the-brim,
shoved his bag in the luggage compartment,
and sat down.

The plane bumped and turned
to head toward the runway
and then revved its engines and headed skyward.

And in the air the plane turned and leveled out,
the landing gear whirred and thumped,
and they flew west.

He needed a shower, maybe two showers,
so he got up and walked to the head,
whose door lay directly
in front of him and the other passengers.

Inside he wet a wad of paper towels,
pulled up his shirt and pulled down his pants,
so that he could wipe himself down with cold water,
a cowboy bath.

Just then someone opened the door,
and he looked down through the plane
at the passengers who had a clear view
of him and his central coast.

So he tipped his cowboy hat
and closed the door.

His exit of the head
was an exercise
in bravery.

JIM'S ADVICE

An Elegy for Jim Harrison

Part I

Somehow, Jones had started writing
letters to the famous writer, Jim,
and getting letters from him in return.

Now twenty-five years later,
Jim had died while he was sitting at his desk
in Patagonia writing a poem.
A good way to go, Jones thought,
if there is a good way to go.

Jones didn't remember how
he'd even gotten Jim's address,
but he'd gotten it, somehow.

He'd met Jim in Key West.
Jones had gone to a bar called
The Green Parrot
that a friend had told him was a place
where the locals hung out,
not a tourist bar like the bars on Duval Street.

And it was a very good place,
since they'd met Frank,
the journalist, there,
who'd ended up getting them both
into damn near every event
that the symposium was having.

One night Jones was in The Green Parrot
drinking and dancing to reggae music with a nice
woman from Arizona that he'd met the night before.

Jim walked in and stood talking
to someone he knew at the bar.
He wore a black sport coat
and Levi's and cowboy boots.

And he was smoking a cigarette, as always.

Jones had read Jim's books and liked them.
Respected them.

"Can I buy you a glass of wine?" Jones asked him.
"Sure, please do," Jim said, his blind eye askew.

Later that week,
he'd been at a party where Jim was telling
someone how he'd gone fly-fishing
for big-game fish off the coast of Ecuador.

"How do you fly-fish in the ocean?" Jones asked him.
"You just put a huge fly on the line and you rear back
and heave that baby as far out there as you can," Jim said,
rearing back and heaving an imaginary fly across the patio.

Two days later,
Jones and his brother were near
a place called The Audubon house
where Jim was going to read some of his poems.
But they needed tickets and had none,
since they'd been sneaking into all the talks
and readings and discussions

that the invited writers were giving that week
with Frank the journalist.

Jim came walking up in his cowboy boots
with a pile of books and papers under his arm.
"Mr. H.," Jones said, "can you get us into your reading?
We don't have tickets."
"The Jones brothers," Jim said.
"Good memory," Jones said.
"Can't seem to forget anything," Jim said and laughed.
"I'll get you in. Hell," he said, "I must've gone to
sixty Lakers games with Jack Nicholson and
they never once asked us for our tickets."

At the table at the entrance
where three gray-haired ladies
were taking the tickets,
one of the women there said,
"Oh my, Mr. H., you know that you shouldn't smoke.
Cigarettes are very bad for you."

So Jim said, "Ma'am, the American Indians
have been smoking tobacco for hundreds of years
and that's the least of their problems."

It had been a great time in Key West for both
Jones and his brother, also named Jones.
They'd run around from reading to bar to discussion
and back to the bar,
and smoked contraband Havana cigars.

And they'd met Jim.

Part II

So twenty-five years later,
when Jim fell from his chair dead,
Jones remembered that time in Key West
and some other times in Montana and L. A.
and the advice that Jim had given him
when he'd gotten together with him,
or written him, or talked on the phone:

"Depression is fly-fishing in dry arroyo;
just keep casting . . ."

"Watch a lot of basketball to avoid the abyss . . ."

"Don't worry
about your son stowing away
on that cruise ship to Mexico;
at least he's not sitting in a shopping mall
with his thumb up his ass . . ."

"Don't worry about the 132 acres that you
almost bought in the Santa Lucia Mountains;
you never really own land anyway;
you just borrow it . . ."

"Steer clear of Green Mojave rattlesnakes,
their bite can kill a two thousand-pound draft horse . . ."

"Drink plenty of French wine
and you'll have dreams about lovely Tahitian wahines . . ."

"Fly fish at least three days a week
so you don't lose your touch and go insane . . ."

"Consider the Yellowstone River my river
since I just let those other people use it out of kindness . . ."

"Eat at gourmet restaurants whether you can afford them or not . . ."

"Drink plenty of expensive vodka
to keep your memories intact and your breath sweet. . ."

"Walk your dogs three hours a day
and keep them close the rest of the time:
they're your only true and unforgiving friends . . ."

"Watch *Columbo* reruns late at night
when you're feeling low . . ."

"If you aren't having fun writing,
go to a good movie or try being an abstract painter,
like Diebenkorn or Rothko . . ."

"Drive twenty-five miles per hour
on country roads so that you don't kill rabbits,
deer, moose, skunks or yourself . . ."

"When you make a lot of money,
spend it all on wine and dinner for your friends
so that you'll never go without wine and dinner later,
and so you will also keep working . . ."

When in Paris eat at Café Select
and drink good Pastis so that you have visions
of expatriates and artists from the twenties
that look like they're from Picasso's Blue Period . . ."

"Always talk to birds, especially ravens,
when you encounter them so they'll give you
very necessary advice when you really need it some day . . ."

"Remember that you are a reincarnated white buffalo
that was a Sioux warrior in a previous life . . ."

"Always carry a pocketknife that has
a screw-driver blade and a corkscrew . . ."

"Never admit to your philandering or your indiscretions,
especially to your wife or your girlfriend . . ."

"When in Arles stay at the Hotel Gran Nord Pinuf
so that you have a view of the canopied café that Van Gogh painted . . ."

"Avoid Republicans so that you don't have to
shoot them later on with your Winchester . . ."

"Bathe in volcano-heated water in Iceland
so that you can meet beautiful,
Icelandic women in those ice-blue pools . . ."

"Never eat surstrømming in Sweden on Swedish holidays
or you'll smell like fermented herring that has sloshed
around in the bilge of a Viking ship for three months . . ."

"In New Zealand, avoid eating creamed corn on toast . . ."

"Don't suffer fools, especially those big assholes
who are worse than a dozen hemorrhoids . . ."

Jones was always careful to follow Jim's wise advice.

HALLOWEEN

We have been carving pumpkins since we
came south from Oregon forty years ago.
Even before the kids.

Marcia gets a sharpie and draws the starburst eyes,
the Doris Day nose,
the smile like Mona Lisa.

Our son carves his pumpkin
as if he is Willem De Kooning
making a mask from a drunk's nightmare.

I get a knife and start cutting,
first the jagged top,
then the angry eyes,
a triangle for the nose,
the jagged mouth an orange face
from a Kafka story.

It looks like an evil politician.

After sunset the kids come to our door.

A five-year-old girl
dressed as a princess says,
"The pumpkins scare me."

A kid dressed as our president
comes to the door.

He has an orange face,
orangutan hair and he's wearing a red tie.

We don't give him any candy.

JACK, GOURMET CHEF

That Summer after Maria and Jack married,
he rented a villa on a hill in Tuscany with nine bedrooms.
He invited eighteen of their friends and relatives to stay there for
free.

(Jack was very rich and he didn't mind spending 60k on people that
he loved and liked.)

Every day at the villa he went to the market,
bought the food,
came back to the villa and cooked a gourmet meal for dinner.
All that he did in Tuscany was cook at the villa, and he loved it.
He had sauce cooking on the stove that he used over and over,
and it was wonderful.

He liked people praising his cooking,
and he liked to control the menu, I think.

There was a bit of the preacher in Jack.
He liked to be the guru that people looked up to,
and occasionally he would make a speech at dinner
about the various people there, and their varied expertise—
writers, filmmakers, professors, experts in financial matters,
whatever else he could drum up to make people feel appreciated.

At dinner, someone said,
"This is wonderful lasagna, Jack. How did you make it?"
"It's a family secret," Jack said.
"Whose family?' his son said.

"A family of one," Jack said.
He didn't tell anyone his recipes at the villa, ever.

One night in California Jack cooked a few dozen clams,
and they were exquisite.

"These are the best clams that I've had in my life," I said.
"How did you make them?"
Maria said, "Jack never gives out his recipes, remember?"
"Hold it," Jack said, "I want to tell Ray how I cook clams."

He told me that there were jalapenos that had to be prepared
a certain way, and you had to have some good white wine,
and you had to have some cherry tomatoes that you put
in the sauce, using no water, just the white wine and garlic,
and, of course, Old Bay, the magic spice.

For some reason Jack wanted to give me the recipe.
Who knows why? Maybe he just wanted to give me a gift.

Jack died a few months later, sad to say.

I'd say exactly how much of this,
and how to do that to cook the clams,
but I don't give out my recipes to just anyone.

CENTAUR

Mick and Jim and Ryan cruised the Westside
in a blue lowered Chevrolet at midnight.
They all wore blue sweatshirts
with Centaur on the back in gold embroidered letters.
Centaur was on the rear window in gold decals, too.

Mick, the driver, turned right at the light.

A turquoise-and-white Ford
rolled toward them out of the dark alley,
then slowed down for a second as a blonde guy
riding shotgun stuck a black pistol out the window.

They were two guys who had just started
a club called Apollos.
They wore blue sweatshirts with Apollos
on the back in gold embroidered letters.

There was a flash and a bang from a pistol.
Mick heard the two in the car laughing as the Ford sped off,
their tires squealing, and Jim, riding shotgun,
saw the name Apollos in gold letters on the rear window.

Mick pulled over to the curb.

He expected blood.

"Is everyone all right?" he said.
Jim, who was riding shotgun said,
"I'm fine. I know those guys.
It was those Apollos dudes, Louie Hertz and Steve Scanlon. "
"No apparent damage," Ryan said from the backseat.
"Those stinking bastards," Mick said.
"First they steal our colors, then they shoot at us."

Mick turned the car around and chased after them,
driving fast for two blocks,
then slow through the dark backstreets
of their neighborhood west of the L. A. River.
The Chevrolet crept down street after street
looking for the Ford and the two guys.

Nothing that way.

Nothing the other way.

Jim knew where the two guys lived,
so they drove by both of their houses
but the Ford wasn't there or it was in a garage.
"They're in American history class at Summer School,
so we'll go and see them tomorrow."

* * *

At eleven the next morning,
eight Centaur cars drove to the high school
and parked out in front in the red.

Mick and Jim and and Ryan
pulled up in the blue Chevrolet,

and they saw the turquoise and white
Ford parked down the block.

Mick and Jim and Ryan got out
and went into the high school building
where they held history classes in the summer.

They found the American history class
and they waited outside in the hall until the bell rang
and the two Apollos from the night before came out.

"You'll want to come with us," Mick said.
"We want to talk to you about last night."
"It was only blanks," Steve, the one who had shot the gun, said.
"It was only a joke."
"Blanks? It was only a joke?" Mick said.
"It wasn't very funny."
"Let's go," Jim said.

They all walked out of the building
to the Chevrolet and the other cars.

All of the Centaur guys
stood beside their cars, waiting.

Mick opened the back door and looked at them.

Steve and Louie got in the back seat.

Jim got in to sit on their left side near the window,
Ryan on their right side.
Mick the driver got in behind the wheel
and they drove north to a two-story white house on a golf course.

19

The eight cars parked.

"After you," Mick said.
"What are you going to do to us?" Steve the shooter asked.
"You'll see," Mick said.

Mick and Ryan and Jim followed the two
into the backyard that overlooked the golf course.

The others Centaurs followed them.

"Have a seat," the driver said.
They sat on a bench near a pond full of orange and white koi fish.

"They were only blanks," Steve the shooter said.
"What are you going to do to us?" he said.
"You'll see," Mick said. "You'll see."

The twelve from the Centaurs stood there
without speaking while looking at the two for thirty minutes.

"Okay," Mick said, "start walking home."
The nine Centaur cars followed them
down the street to Steve's house,
then down another street to Louie's house.

All through the summer
a different Centaur car followed them
in the morning and then after class,
one car or another drove slowly behind them.

Steve and Louie would remember that summer
seeing the Centaur cars in the mirror
following them for the rest of their lives.

Who would forget it?

A STARCHED WHITE SHIRT IN WAIKIKI

I spent my last five dollars
on a haircut and a plate lunch,
then walked to the gas station
where I applied for a job.

I looked clean-cut, I guess,
so they hired me.

We wore starched white uniforms
with starched white hats
and a phony bow-tie
that clipped onto our starched collars.

It was eighty-five and humid
and it made no sense to
wear a bow-tie and a starched shirt
but the company wanted us to look like the posters.

The manager held a contest about
who sold the most tires,
oil changes, or windshield wipers,
and so forth.

Each of us had a paper rocketship
that pointed toward the heavens on their graph.

I always opened my top button
on that starched shirt and let
my bow-tie dangle from the collar

so that the air cooled my neck
while I pumped gas or changed the oil.

I sold a lot of tires and oil changes
but I didn't like the contest
so I gave a Hawaiian guy all of my sales so that his
rocketship could climb toward the heavens.

He won a weekend on the North Shore and a toaster.

*   *   *

When I quit to go to Kauai the station manager said,
"You're one of those guys who will just drift around
from job to job for your whole life
and have nothing to show for it."

"Maybe so," I said.
"Maybe I won't be wearing a starched shirt and a bow-tie
and working in an Oahu gas station when I'm sixty."

On Kauai I rented a three-fifty a day room
at the Kobayama Hotel and looked with no success
for waves to bodysurf.

One afternoon I met some Norwegian
Merchant Marines in a bar on Nawiliwili Bay.
They knew all about drifting from place to place.

BEING HERE AND BEING THERE AND EVERYWHERE

When Zee is up at the cabin in the woods of Idaho
on the Canadian border away from the beach
he remembers the Pacific Ocean breeze coming
up the avenue past his house in the afternoons down South.

Here are a few other things he misses:

Driving over the suspension bridge above
the harbor into San Pedro.

The green sailboat, her new, Sitka Spruce bowsprit
that's painted with twelve coats of varnish.

Running South on a light wind on a reach headed North.

Warm ocean around him as he bodysurfs
a five-foot wave toward shore, then flipping out.

The spindrift off a wave that sprays his face
during a Santa Ana wind.

Watching *Columbo* as Peter Falk chews his cigar
and wondering why the detective always wears
that London Fog raincoat even though it never rains.

Marcia coming home from working someone's garden,
dirt and mud on the butt of her pants.

The bookstore where there's
a long shelf of Harrison books and
also a long shelf of Bukowski books.

The store down the coast that sells
his English tobacco and that good wine.

Smoking a Honduran cigar
while driving home along the coast.

Driving to the desert in December to see John,
who always smiles even though he's always sick.

His brother Steve coming by the house
and fixing his computer or TV as if it's nothing.

His son coming home and drinking a Heineken or two
while sitting near the fire-pit in the backyard
as he listens to Bob Dylan and Hoagy Carmichael.

Their mist-green California bungalow.

The raw fir frames of the inside windows
rubbed with Watco and tung oil.

The leather easy chair where Zee can sit
and look out the high window
to see the top of the fifty-foot tall palm tree's fronds
moving back and forth in the wind.

Zee's brother, Tony, standing on the bow of the sailboat
as they sail through still water in the channel of the bay.

Lunch with Leo, drinking a pint or two of root beer
at Joe Josts then eating a Special with onions and a pickled egg.

Talking to friends who know things about books and movies.

A kid in a class who gets excited about reading
and writing stories and the surprise about his loving it.

Sipping an espresso with a squirt of chocolate
and some cream and sitting at the café on the marina
while watching the people walk by to the market.

Frank Sinatra on the jazz station on Sunday mornings.

Trying to solve The Times chess problem
about white mating black in just two moves.

He doesn't miss:

The Harley chopper roaring across town.

The guy in the market parking lot
playing a song about big butts.
The woman pushing her newborn ahead of her
in a baby carriage and yelling at her four-year-old.

Actually, Zee feels very good when he's back.

He likes going eighty miles an hour on the freeway
with the rest, like two hundred pelicans in formation.

But he keeps the screened door locked to avoid ladrones,
and keeps his machete lying within reach beside the front door.

When Zee thinks of the cabin in the woods he misses:

The moose mother and baby that sleep in the tall grass out front.

Two thousand-and-two Canadian Geese
flying in large Vs home above the Kootenay River at dusk.

Fishing on the Yaak River in Montana,
even though he never catches any fish.

Stopping at Marv the Cowboy's cabin and drinking
a few beers while Marv tells him stories
about the 8,000 horses that he's owned,
broken, doctored and sold in his life.

Of course there are other things that Zee misses
and doesn't miss when he and his wife
are living in either house.

One hell of a lot of things, really.

But in the end, Zee is from the Pacific Coast,
and he loves the smell of the ocean
on the onshore wind on a cool afternoon.

And he knows that a lake or a river
just ain't no ocean.

HORSE SENSE

I have found that if you ever
happen to be on a runaway horse
at a PowWow in Flagstaff, Arizona,
you should turn the horse's head
either left or right and the horse will stop,
since it doesn't care to go in a circle.

Don't pull back and shout, "Whoa,"
since that doesn't work.

Also, it's a good idea
to talk to the horse before you get on
so that you let the horse know
that you are a good guy
who just wants a nice, calm ride.

That's what is called "horse sense."

I hope this is helpful
when you encounter a horse.

SAN FERNANDO

From the ages of fourteen through eighteen,
I went over to Avalon on Catalina Island
in the summers to stay on my friend Richard's boat
(really his father's boat),
The Norseman,
for a month or so.

His parents would let a few of us
stay on The Norseman during the summer.
Richard's family was Portuguese.
His great-grandparents had come to California
in the 1800s because it was a lot like Portugal,
I suppose,
and because it was on the ocean.

(Avalon is a little town on Catalina.
The island is just twenty-two miles long
and is part of a string of islands, the Channel Islands,
off the coast of Southern California.
A lot of Catalina and the other islands in the chain
are still the way that Cabrillo found them in 1542 . . .
. . . except for the environmental damage
to the indigenous flora and fauna by goats
and feral pigs and bison that have been left there
to roam the island by various visitors over the years.)

The Norseman had been a Coast Guard rescue boat.
Its design was like a spindle, rounded off on the top
and on the bottom to keep it afloat in huge seas.

Mr. Costello, Richard's father, had put a mast on her
so she looked almost like a sailboat.

They had her tied to a can off Avalon,
and she was our bedroom.
We survived on almost nothing in those days.
Pancakes in the morning,
a sandwich later on,
a few beers that we would get somehow.

(California then was not like California today.
There was no freeway along the coast, for example,
and you drove south to Tijuana and Ensenada
or north to San Francisco on Pacific Coast Highway,
which was just a two-lane road.)

There was an old man in Avalon
that the locals called San Fernando.
He walked with a cane and wore a blue baseball hat.
His face looked as if it had been twisted
like a Dali clock.

In the early 1900s he and his family had owned
thousands of acres in the San Fernando Valley.

(Everyone has heard of the San Fernando Valley.
It's mentioned in a song that Gene Autry sang long ago—
when the San Fernando Valley was open country,
with ranches here and there, a lot of horses,
and a lot of cowboys like Gene Autry.

That was before WWII, when California was a place
where "people made movies" and the only thing

the rest of the country knew about the state was
that it had a bridge called the Golden Gate in San Francisco.

Then the Second World War came and
millions of men and women from the Midwest and
the rest of the country came out to California
to serve in the Army, Navy or Marines.

After the war, those same people came back to live
in a place where there was really no winter
and there were a lot of jobs,
and the land was pretty cheap if you got a GI Loan.

The San Fernando Valley is now filled with houses and people.
Some of the young women from the San Fernando Valley
are called "Valley Girls" nowadays,
and they're famous for using "like" before every other word
and "awesome" at least once in a paragraph.)

We didn't know much during those years,
but we knew what had happened
to the San Fernando Valley after the war.
The value of the land there had soared because of all
of the people who were migrating there.

*   *   *

Years later, in Avalon, the kids of the island
heard what had happened to the old man
who walked with a cane:

Just before the war broke out, they heard,
he'd sold the thousands of acres that his family owned cheap,

and then retired to Avalon with the paltry
amount of money that he got from that sale.

When the war was over the ex-military guys
began to return to California
to live where there were no winters
and work at some aircraft factory
or start a business and get a house somewhere,
like the San Fernando Valley.

The old man with the cane had made a big mistake,
the biggest mistake of his life.
He'd sold the land to developers cheap at exactly the wrong time.

When the kids in Avalon would see him
walking by with his cane they would yell,
"Hey, San Fernando."
And every time he would say,
"Up the line. Up the line."

Many years later, the day would come
when they would make their big mistake,
something that they would regret doing
for the rest of their lives.

If it didn't happen to them when they were young,
it would happen some time soon enough.

One day they'd be walking with a cane down
the street somewhere,
and some kids would have heard
about that big mistake that they made
somewhere along the line,
and they might yell it out at them.

They'd remember San Fernando
but call their big mistake by another name.

*   *   *

The name of mine is Kay.

You probably know the name of yours.

MARCIA'S MYSTERIOUS WAY OF KNOWLEDGE

It was ten o'clock at night and
a dozen of us sat or stood around the fire
at a place called Saldamando,
where we all often camped
on a beach just north of
Ensenada in Baja.

We were out on a point
above the beach fifteen feet high or so,
with big volcanic boulders
surrounding the tongue of land
where we all talked and laughed.

Everyone had a glass of tequila in hand.
My wife, Marcia, and I as well.
We'd all drunk a lot by then.

My friend Ralph looked across the fire and said,
"We've lost Marcia," and just then
Marcia's distinctive laughter echoed up
from twenty feet down on the beach
beyond the boulders of the tongue
of land we were on.

"How'd you get down there?"
I shouted to her.
"I guess that I just walked off the edge
and got down here somehow."
Her glass of tequila was still in her hand.

"Are you hurt?" I asked.
"No, I don't think so," she said.

I ran down the path to the beach and got to her.

I could see the fire's glow up fifteen feet
above us over the top of the ragged boulders.

"You're sure that you're okay?" I said.
"Yeah, I must've flown down over those
boulders somehow," she said.
"You could've killed yourself," I said,
as I walked her up the hill and back to the fire.
"I know," she said and laughed.

Back again around the fire,
we all talked about the mystery
of her walking through the sky
over the boulders to end up
on the beach without a scratch.

"You must've flown down on your laughter,"
Ralph said.

The glow of the fire reflected
off our faces as we laughed with her,
very glad that she was unscathed.

With the help of tequila,
Doña Marcia can walk
through the sky like a raven.

We all thank the gods of the maguey
for Marcia and her Mysterious Way of Knowledge.

MAVERICK'S

Part I

The Trip

Drove up to Maverick's in Half Moon Bay on Monday
to see the waves (eight hours up and eight hours back).

The contest was canceled yet there were still big waves,
sixty-foot faces "like blue mountains," they said.

The captain of the fishing boat
that we were about to go out to see them on
docked his boat and tied up,
then walked off to the pier.

"The fog was too dense out there," he said.
"I couldn't see the swells of the waves coming
and I couldn't see the rocks to avoid them. Dangerous."

If it's dangerous for the captain,
it's dangerous for everybody, we figured.
So I didn't see anything but dense fog from the point
where the surfers paddled out to disappear into
the thick grey cloud and head toward unseen giants.
But it was an interesting trip, worth the try.

Next time, perhaps, there will be no fog.
That's like a lot of things, isn't it?

Part II

That day as I watched the surfers disappear into the fog,
I thought of the revolutionary in the canyon
who hollered from behind the rocks:

"Listen, when you have no cause you have nothing.
At first, you choose to stay because you believe;

then you leave since you are disillusioned;
then you return because you are lost.

Finally, you die because you are committed."

BLUE AND YELLOW FINS

On Oahu at Makapu'u Beach
he learned to ride the face of the waves right or left,
then cut back and behind the waves as they broke.
Makapu'u's waves usually had six-foot faces,
but often they would roll in with twelve-foot faces
and if you missed turning in time you came down
in white water that was all air and bubbles
with no up and no down.

At Sandy Beach the waves crashed
right down onto the sand.
You took off on the wave late,
so that you could come down on the water
that was the backwash of the previous wave
and that cushioned your fall on to the sand.

At both places he went in without fins,
just as the locals that he learned from did.

No one wore fins then.
They didn't even think of it.
Who knows why?

That was long ago,
when he'd lived in what they called The Jungle,
the slums just behind Waikiki.

The tourists at the Royal Hawaiian
on Waikiki Beach, that pink hotel,
learning to surf on the long

breaking waves and drinking
mai tais and piña coladas.

Many years later,
he could hardly swim without his
blue-and-yellow Churchills.
Those fins let him move fast enough
to catch the wave,
then gave him power enough to dive
and get away from the breaking water
as it crashed toward the shore.

He wondered now what he'd been
thinking back then,
going into waves as big as locomotives,
the blue water crashing down
and turning white.

Of course, some waves didn't
care if you wore fins or not.

They grabbed you and slapped you
around in the white water,
then took you on a riptide
toward some place like the Sargasso Sea,
where people stupid enough to think
that they could always stay safe in any ocean
found out they'd always had it wrong,
and it was way too late to do anything about it.

OUT IN OPEN OCEAN

My brother and I are a good team
when we go sailing on Bacchante,
my thirty-six foot sloop.

He clips the jib to the forestay,
uncovers the mainsail
and fastens the main sheet halyard.

I go below and open the valve
for the gas and the sea water,
then turn the battery switch to on,
start the engine and let it run fast
to warm it up.
Then I unclip the covers
on the dodger's windows
and stow the main sail cover
that my brother has removed.

We have always been good partners
in getting work done.
We each move to do our jobs without talking,
even when we delivered flowers
to weddings and funerals for our folks.

Weddings in churches or chapels
always had an old lady who
told us what to do as we rushed
through our separate jobs,
while not listening to her
as she squawked away.

We brought in the baskets of flowers
and the candleabras,
placed the flowers on either side
of the kneeling bench,
then placed the candelabras
to the left and the right of the flowers,
peeled the cellophane from the candles
and placed the candles to stand up straight,
then began attaching the bows onto every second pew,
from the front of the church, to the back.

*　*　*

Then we brought in the aisle runner,
a long roll of white linen.
One of us went to the back and picked up the roll
then set it down while pulling back
on it to let it roll all of the way
from the back of the church
to the kneeling bench,
where we then hid the end of the roll
that was left over behind the
kneeling bench and pinned down
the cloth on the two stairs.

Sometimes we made it roll all of the way,
and some time it was a little short.

All the while the old lady was chattering
as she watched us decorate in a flash of light—
she with her mouth still going—
we in the truck speeding off
to deliver a casket spray for someone's coffin,
or a corsage for someone's prom.

Now my brother hauls up the mainsail
while we're still in the bay
as we put out through the channel to open ocean,
where he hauls up the jib,
and we sail to the south and leave
all of the squawking behind us.

CADILLAC EL DORADO

Grandma had a mist green,
1957 Cadillac El Dorado
with a brushed, stainless-steel top,
and five-thousand miles on the odometer.

She and her husband Nieto only drove it to mass,
at Saint Anthony's church three blocks from their home.

She always bought the most expensive things
that she could find,
so Nieto had to slave away in the flower shop
all week and all year to make enough money
to pay for her clothes,
her shoes, her furs,
her velvet couches, her crystal chandeliers.

You might say that she was eccentric.

I went north to Oregon in the seventies.
I told my parents,
"Don't let Grandma sell that El Dorado."

One morning back in the fifties
Grandma had the people from the shoe store
come to her house,
where she picked out a pair
of powder-blue high-heeled shoes,
then ordered them in a dozen different colors,
all pastels.

She always wore each pair of her high-heels at least once,
then put them back in a box in her closet
on top of hundreds of other boxes of shoes.

She played her electric player-piano in the living room
once on Christmas Eve and once on her birthday,
the year only a mystery.

In her kitchen she had a white enamel,
chrome-covered Chambers stove with two broilers
and a steamer and two ovens.

Her closet was crammed with clothes
that she had bought and never used—
full-length gowns of white, black, blue and pink,
eight fur coats from now extinct animals.

When she died,
my parents piled her un-scuffed shoes,
still in their boxes,
five feet high along the wall
of her French rococo living room.

My uncle brought the velvet couch,
the chrome-covered stove,
and the electric player piano to my house,

and I put the couch and the stove in our garage,
and the piano in the front room
where I planned to fix its electric motor.

Last week, after twenty years,
we sold the velvet couch for a hundred dollars

and put the old stove on the curb
for some scrap-metal man to pick up.

My son is making a Keinholtz-like sculpture out of the piano.

When I was still in Oregon,
two old men had knocked on her door and asked her
if she wanted to sell the Cadillac.

Somehow they'd heard about the El Dorado parked in her garage.

She said, "Si. You want comprarlo.
Es muy dirty and dusty now.
You clean it, not me, okay?"

They gave her nine-hundred dollars for the car,
put some oil in the cylinders through the spark-plug holes,
jumped the battery, started it up, and drove it away
on white sidewall tires that were still just like new.

She liked the feel of the money in her hand.

When my parents went to clean out her house,
they hung the clothes on racks in the living room.
Most of them vintage dresses and suits
that were now antiques worth good money to the right people.

In order to clear the house of so many things,
my folks sold them to a woman from Hollywood
who wanted the suits and dresses to use in movies
set in the twenties, thirties, forties and fifties.

She paid my parents eight-hundred dollars for everything.

Nieto, who had become her second husband in California
after my father's father died in Mexico,
had paid many thousands of dollars for the lot.

Grandma would have loved to know
that the clothes went to Hollywood.

She loved the movie stars and had pictures
of Lucille Ball and Marilyn Monroe,
her heroes,
sitting in gold frames on the dresser in her bedroom.

The green-and-silver El Dorado,
worth two or three hundred thousand now,
sits in a showroom full of classic cars up in Lake Tahoe.

People walk up and touch its subtle fins,
run their fingers over its metallic-green body.

"What year is it?" one man says.
"A '57," says another.

"What a lovely green color," a woman says,
"Who do you think owned it?" she asks.

"Probably a movie star," another man says,
"or some very eccentric millionaire."

LORRAINE AROUND?

I was sitting in a café with a screenwriter
and I said, "Old Bukowski's gone."

And the screenwriter said, "Yeah,
I have a funny story about him."

"Me too," I said. "I met him one time
and later on I was sitting in a bar
where he was going to read,
and he walked by me and looked over and said,
'Oh oh, someone let the Mexicans in.'"

"I think that he was a good writer," the screenwriter said.

I said, "I do too, as a matter of fact,
but that was what he said.
I'm not sensitive about being Mexican."

"Oh," the screenwriter said and looked over at me.
"I was living in this place in L. A.
and I had the phone number of some woman
that Bukowski knew way back,
and at three in the morning he called
and said, 'Lorraine around?'

And I said, 'There's no Lorraine here.'
And he said, 'Are you sure about that?'
And I said, 'Yeah, I'm sure.'

But he kept calling about
twice a week for a month,
and he was drunk at 3 a.m.

I knew his voice, and I knew it was him,
and I finally said, 'Mr. Bukowski,
there's no Lorraine here.
I am sorry about that but I have to get some sleep,
so please cross that number out of your book.

I'd like to talk to you some time earlier
in the evening, perhaps.
Put Roy next to that number if you want.'

He said, 'Very sorry to bother you, Roy.
But I would really like to get ahold of Lorraine tonight.
You won't be hearing from me again.
I'm not much at calling one of my pals
at three o'clock in the morning.'"

CAN THIS WOLF SURVIVE?

He smelled coffee and tea, then alcohol, as well as urine mixed with shit, all of those spores of things that drifted around him there from the hallway, as he lay in bed in the hospital, the bed adjusted to the sitting position like a lazy U, the television's smell of hot parts filling the room. He'd had chemotherapy to shrink the tumor that was as big as an apple in his colon. He'd sat in a Lazy Boy chair two days a week for months as the poison had dripped into his veins. He'd had radiation to burn the tumor and shrink it. Doctor Hertzog, the radiologist, said, You might lose a kidney from the radiation. And the patient told him, I would like to keep that kidney, if possible. He said, I like that kidney a lot. Dr. Hertzog said, Okay, I'll avoid it for you somehow. You're very nonchalant about my kidney, he said. You have two of them, Dr. Hertzog said. After all that he had surgery, performed by a surgeon who had the aura of a jet pilot combined with the skill of a Samurai. Then as he lay in the hospital bed he smelled rotten flesh, the iron of blood, pus, alcohol, urine, feces, sweat, disinfectant, deodorant, moisturizing lotion, and just about every other thing there was to smell as he stumbled out of his bed and walked down the hallways to encounter as yet unknown odors. A doctor friend and his wife came to visit. They stood beyond the foot of his bed, and he asked, Did you enjoy your fish dinner? How do you know that we had a fish dinner? they asked. I can smell the fish, he said. It was halibut from Alaska. They laughed, thinking he was joking. They told him, You're very weird. It must be the morphine, they said. When he got out of the hospital and got strong enough to get out in the world again, he and his wife got in his old Mercedes diesel. They drove the freeway inland to the city to see a Cezanne exhibition. The diesel smell made him nauseous as he recalled it had done years ago when he sat, fishing pole in hand, in a boat that bobbed up and down in a

55

consistent pattern of gentle swells that rolled into the little bay near the village of San Felipe, in Baja. He'd smelled the gasoline from the cars as well as the odor of the injured alveoli in his lungs. He'd smelled the gasoline's molecules as they burned his nostrils. At the Cezanne exhibit they entered the room where the paintings were, and he stood alone just three feet from a painting of two card players, and he smelled the oil paint that had been applied to the canvas over a hundred years ago. He smelled the turpentine and the Japanese drier that Cezanne had mixed with his oil paint. He moved to another painting and stood next to a man of thirty-five or so who wore clean khaki shorts, a button-down, plaid shirt, and brand new white tennis shoes. The painting that he and the man in shorts looked at was of a hill or a mountain in Provence. The painting was almost Cubist because of Cezanne's brushstrokes. The man beside him was clean-shaven, with a fresh haircut, and the aroma of the barber's aftershave lotion, but he also reeked of shit, so he moved to stand beside a young, tidy woman in a gray business suit, as they viewed a painting of a stand of trees, and she, also, smelled as if she hadn't wiped herself properly. Then he moved to where he could look at a painting of blue and green and brown apples on a table, where a prim old lady with blue-gray hair came to stand next to him, and her pungent perfume mixed with the smell of urine was even worse than the shit of the others. He found his wife and told her, I can't stand it in here any longer today. I'll wait for you outside. It had not been a pleasant exhibition so far even though he loved the paintings and their paint and turpentine smell, but he saw no chance of it getting any better. In the car on the way home, his wife laughed at him and said, You have a wolf's nose. It will pass, she said, in a month or two. This is not a pleasant thing to have, he said, this acute ability to smell like a wolf. He felt sympathy for wolves and dogs and elephants. What must they smell? he said. How can they stand it? he said. He remembered how it was in Sweden many years ago when he had smelled their Surstrømming, the fermented mackerel that the Swedes somehow were able to eat on special occasions. It's left over from something that our Viking ancestors ate, they said, something that they had to eat on their long voyages. It's just like the mackerel that sloshed around in the bilges of their ships for many months. It smells like vomit, he thought, on the first day that the Swedish students at the university had eaten it. The smell had lingered outside of those students' doorways when he walked by for several weeks. What can I do? I'm cursed to smell the cheap perfume, cologne, yesterday's onions, garlic and shit of fat women and men who've pissed their pants and now surround me on the street. Where can I go? The forest? The jungle? Out to sea? Outer space? Up higher into mountain air? These are questions that he still asks himself every morning when he smells the fresh milk-like odor of the beautiful Incan woman with her long black hair and elegant stride as she walks by the café where he sits beside the cobblestone street that runs through the village where he smells the old man who sits beside him smoking a Havana cigar as the old man sips his espresso in this café at twelve-thousand feet. Will her smell be as pleasant tomorrow? he asks. He sips the maté that smells of wild grasses, through a bent, tin straw, and asks himself, Where else can I go from here? He asks, can this wolf survive?

OUR FRIEND RITA

Paul drove his brand-new red pickup
the last mile to my friend Watson's place
in Arizona and I said,
"There's one thing that you have to be careful of
at Watson and Rita's.
Rita always pulls A Rita, so just watch out."

"What's A Rita?" Paul asked.
"Don't worry," I said, "you'll find out."

Rita was a Navajo, like Watson, my friend of fifty years.
She always loved the soap operas
and she had her hair cut short
and styled with blonde streaks in it
just like an actress that she liked on t.v.

We drove into the yard up to the open garage door
where Watson stood smiling, a can of beer in his hand.

He spent most of his time in that garage,
making silver bracelets and rings,
or tinkering with cars or machinery
while he drank his beer to then throw the empty cans
into a blue plastic barrel in the corner.

We got out of Paul's red pickup,
and Watson said, "Hey brother, it's good to see you,"
then took my hand and gave me a hug.

"Good to see you, too, Watson," I said.
I introduced Paul to him and they shook hands.

"We'll have to go fishing tomorrow," Watson said.
"We'll go up to Reservation Lake and catch a few trout."

That night we ate steaks and beans
and drank the beer that I'd bought at the market,
and in the morning we put the fishing poles
in the back of Watson's pickup
and just as we were getting in to drive away

Rita said, "Do you mind if I drive your pickup a little, Paul?"

"Sure," Paul said,
"go ahead and take her for a little spin,"
and handed her the keys.

"Okay," she said, "thanks."

I looked over at Paul but said nothing,
then we headed down the road toward Reservation Lake
on the Apache Reservation, fifty miles south.

When we got there we fished the lake for a while
from the bank and looked around
at the lodgepole pine forest all around the lake.

Besides us there were only a couple of Apaches
there who ran a little bait store
with a dock out front where they had
three aluminum boats to rent.

We didn't catch a thing in the lake, but it was a good day anyway.

So when we drove in to Watson's yard that night
Paul's pickup was gone and when we went inside
Watson's daughter Tammy was the only one there.

"Mom drove Paul's pickup somewhere at about noon," she said.
"Where'd she go?" Watson said.
"She didn't say where she was going," Tammy said.

So we drank a few beers and waited two hours
in the garage until up drove Rita with a dozen
or more bales of hay stacked high in the back
of Paul's pickup.

"Where'd you get the hay?" Watson said.
"I went down to Phoenix and got it," she said.
"It's a dollar a bale cheaper down there."

"Isn't Phoenix a hundred and fifty miles away?" I said.
"A little bit less," Rita said and went inside.

Paul didn't say anything for a while, then he said,
"Let's go somewhere and have a beer."
"You go ahead," Watson said.
"I need to talk to Rita about something."

There was a bar down the highway half a mile,
and we drove there in Paul's pickup,
him silent and stern-faced.

When we got inside the bar and sat down,
we ordered two beers and Paul told the woman behind the bar,
"Give me a shot of your good tequila."

Then he took his cowboy hat off
and set it on the bar and drank the tequila
and chased it with a beer.

"This morning there was a full tank of gas in the pickup," he said,
"and now there's just a quarter tank."

"I told you about looking out for A Rita," I said,
"and that was A Pure Rita if I ever saw one."

"Yes," he said, and sipped his tequila,
"I guess it was."

RASHOMON **REVISITED**

The young woman came into my office,
her nostrils flaring.

She was in my writing class
and she hadn't attended for a couple of weeks.

"I need to drop your class," she said.

"That's too bad," I said.
"It's the seventh week. The semester's half done.
Are you having some problems?"

"Well, yes . . . I don't like the way that you think
about LGBT people."

"What are you talking about?" I asked.

"You said that gay people have sex with animals."

"I never said that," I said.
"Yes, you did," she said.
"You said that gay people screw buffaloes."

"Wait a minute," I said.
"You're talking about the story I told in class
about what my gay friend, Tom,
said to a young guy that he'd met in a bar."

I had told a story in class about my friend, Tom,
who had met a young guy in a bar

and he'd asked him what he did,
and the young guy'd said
that he was a Creative Writing major at State.

So my friend had asked him how it was going,
and the young guy had said that he was worried,
that he was taking a short story writing class,
and that he didn't know about the professor,
that he was a gruff guy who looked like a truck driver.

And he'd described the guy as having dark hair,
stocky, with a weird Spanish name.

So my friend had said, "That's my neighbor Ray.
He wouldn't even care if you wanted to screw buffalos."

"My friend Tom said that about buffalos.
He said that I wouldn't care 'if' someone wanted to screw
buffalos," I said.
"My friend said 'if,' not 'that.'"

"Oh," she said..

 "You might reconsider dropping," I said. "Think about it."

"Maybe," she said.

So the young woman dropped the class anyway.

Wars have been declared over lesser things.

BLUE AND YELLOW FINS II

On Oahu when he was nineteen he'd started body-surfing the right way, the way that Hawaiians did it. Back in California, he'd been out on a board at Trestle, where the Marines often chased them off, and at Dana Point, when the break rolled around the left of the point like a six-handed clock toward shore. He was just learning to board-surf there on the mainland, but then he flew to Oahu, with no board and little money; just a pair of canvas trunks, no towel and no fins.

He was broke, lucky to eat a bowl of saimin, or some Jungle Stew made of hamburger and canned vegetables and rice that that they ate there in the White House in the area filled with old houses that sat behind Waikiki's beach, called The Jungle at the time. They lived there one block behind the big pink hotel on the beach, where the tourists lay on the sand and drank their mai tais and piña coladas.

He'd landed on the island with two hundred dollars, and two months later, he spent his last five dollars on a mahi mahi-and-rice plate-lunch with soy sauce and a haircut. With that, he got a job pumping gas in Waikiki. By that time he'd gone body-surfing daily with some of the locals and a couple of friends from the mainland. It was free entertainment, something that the money changers couldn't figure out a way to get paid for yet.

Some locals showed him which swell to choose and how to get into a wave's shoulder and slide right or left, how to kick out before the wave broke on your head, how to stay out of trouble at Makapu'u or Sandy Beach.

All of them had gone in to the water without fins back then. "Wearing fins is cheating," they said. "They make it too easy." He wasn't a strong swimmer, but he got better, learning how to stay alive when a ten-foot wave—or even a three-foot wave—slapped him around like he was in some giant's washing machine.

He did okay, riding the shoulders left or right with his back bowed and his right or left hand a rudder in the wave's face, so that the wave spit him out to where he could roll forward, then back and behind the wave, out of the soup. Of course, sometimes he was crushed by falling water, flailing around in a swirl of white foam and bubbles where he didn't know which way was up. Sometimes that was the way of things.

He went out into some dragon-sized waves later, riding them toward shore, then coming out as if he was shipwrecked to lie face down on the wet sand where he thanked the Hawaiian gods for letting him live to see another wave.

One afternoon, decades later, when he was in the water on the mainland, he wore a pair of blue-and-yellow rubber fins, and he got into a wave easily, slid right, and then kicked out and over to safety. Then he got into a spot where the fins got him under the face of a wave that was too late to ride, then out of a swirling rip that was taking him for a ride out to where the sea monsters lived.

He thought, What was I doing back then? Those waves would have been so much easier to handle if I'd worn fins in the water. Of course, by then there had been so many times and situations when he'd gone into dangerous water, without fins, that it was like counting the stars in the Milky Way.

By then he knew that sometimes it was just like he was in the water without fins, whether he wore fins in or not. Some waves just did with you whatever they wanted to do. They were wild horses at the Gates of Hades just arriving on a hurricane from Hawaii.

CARELESS

"Where's my pipe? Where are my keys?" he said. "I must've lost a hundred pipes over the years. Well, at least I'm not accident-prone, like Frank, who trips over his own feet and has a way of finding yellow-jacket nests wherever he goes even though he's allergic to bees. He has to carry around a kit with the antidote in it so that he can give himself a shot to keep him from going into shock. He's a damn magnet for yellow-jackets." His wife says, "You're careless and forgetful. I'm afraid to let you take the dog to the beach because you might lose her or leave her behind." He says, "I'm not going to lose the dog." She says, "Where's the mail? Did you throw it out again?" And he says, "I'll look at the stuff that I put in the recycle bin to make sure." "Please," she says. "Yeah, here's that check you were looking for," he says, and she says, "See, you're sooo careless." "Here's that bill from the insurance company as well," he says, "but we paid that, didn't we?" "No," she says, "we didn't pay it yet." "Where's my pipe?" he says. "You left it on the coffee table, so the puppy ate it," she says. "Oh, well, there are a lot of pipes out there, I guess," he says. "But I liked that pipe. No, here it is. That must've been something else that the puppy chewed up." She says, "Jesus, that was that hand-carved statuette that I got in the Black Forest when I was five. You were messing around with it last night and you left that on the coffee table, I guess." He reaches into his back pocket to get his tobacco pouch. "Crap, it looks like I lost another tobacco pouch." She says, "At least you make your own, so that's no big loss." He says, "Shit, it's late. I have to go to the bank. Where are my damn keys?" "I give up," she says. "Use mine."

132 ACRES UP ON THE COAST

I

The 132 acres of land
sat at the top of a long valley,
and it was for sale.

The valley ran downhill and ended at the sea,
and from the winding road at the top
you could see the sun shining on the ocean
five miles down the hill.

The only stream that brought water to the town
at the mouth of the valley began from two springs
that started the stream near the top of the hill
on that land.

The couple called and asked how much it cost,
and it was a lot,
but just about as much as the average house
where they lived two hundred miles to the south.

II

A road ran along the top of the land,
and a plateau at the top was a good place to build a house.

So they went to a bank,
and it happened that the loan officer at the bank
knew a good friend of theirs.

The friend had helped the loan officer
to take a class he'd needed to graduate from college,
so the banker was thankful.

The couple waited for the bank's decision,
and after a week the banker said, "Yes, you can afford it."

They were amazed that their assets
were good enough yet they started the process
to buy the land and it began to go through escrow.

III

A Spanish family owned the land.
Old Californians.

They'd owned it for three hundred years;
it had been part of a Spanish land grant.

Thirty sons and daughters and cousins were involved,
since it'd been handed down from
many siblings to their children,
then to their children, and so on.

All thirty had to accept the offer that the couple made,
and they would divvy up 750 thousand dollars,
which would cost the couple six thousand dollars a month.

Because the loan was just for empty land,
the loan was good for only two years,
when the bank would want to see
if there had been any improvements
so that the loan might then be accepted again
and be processed for a longer time.

IV

The man knew that they couldn't afford all of the land,
in the long run.

They'd use up all of their money after those two years.

They'd need a partner that would buy half of the land.

There was another flat hilltop where someone
could put a house down the hill a ways.

V

The man and the woman walked the land
with their son and daughter
and walked through a grove of oak trees,
with a bed of leaves that was as big as a football field.

Down the hill boulders had holes made
many hundreds of years back by the Chumash Indians
for grinding pine nuts, or "metates."

VI

A small house was up the hill from the land
so they drove up to see who lived there.

The man there had lived in the valley
for twenty years.

He'd built his house there.

"It's beautiful here," he said,

"but watch out for those green Mojaves
when you walk through that tall grass.
 They can kill a thousand pound horse . . .

Around sunset it's a good idea
to carry a .45 because the mountain lions
are out looking for food at that time.

The rattlers come up in hay
from the desert."

VII

The sixty days of the escrow raced along to thirty days.

The woman doing the escrow got all thirty
of the signatures from the Spanish family
after a lot of work.

VIII

The man got in touch with
a friend who had some money,
then walked the land with him,
thinking that the friend
might go in half with them.

The friend said, "It's spectacular.
But I'm done with buying land;
for now I'm renting.

Anyway, I don't like the idea of
Green Mojaves slithering around in the tall grass,

or those mountain lions
prowling around at sunset."

VIV

One day the man called the escrow office;
the friendly woman who'd worked like hell
and gotten all of the signatures
had been fired for being too slow.

X

The man and the woman were
having nightmares about the land,
about living there in a teepee
or a pup tent since they didn't know
where they'd get money
to build a house on the land.

Their money would all be gone
after two years of payments,
so they'd have to give the land to the bank.

XI

"What were we thinking when we got into this?"
the woman said.

"I can't get to sleep from worrying about it,
and when I do my nightmares wake me up,
and I'm sweating."

So they called and dropped out of escrow,
told them that the deal was off,

and got their five-thousand dollar deposit back,
even though the owners could
have kept it if they'd wanted to.

XII

Then the man and woman slept better.
But they dreamed about the land,
because it was one of the most beautiful places
that they'd ever seen.

So the woman said,
"It was a privilege just to walk around on that place.
It should be a national park it's so beautiful."

XIII

Now when they travel north along the coast,
they drive up the winding road along the stream
to the top of the valley,

and they look down to the sea across
the still empty land and think
that the Green Mojaves and the mountain lions
have it and they didn't have to pay the bank anything at all.

SHARKS

Dave had been my friend for
fifteen years when he died.

And for all of those years
he had always been late to his classes,
late to golf,
late to the nine o'clock movie.

He went into a theatre in the multiplex
and sat there for ten minutes,
checked out the lighting,
then left to go down the hall
to the next movie where he sat
for ten minutes and again
looked at the lighting,
then left to move down the hall
to the next movie.

He was on
"Dave Time,"
we called it,
always moving,
always heading off to somewhere else
to see or do something,

like seeing the leaves change
to orange in Autumn in Illinois.

He didn't care about the story
of a movie or the acting,
just the lighting.

He made abstract films
that were more like paintings by Rauschenberg
than like films by Ford or Kurosawa.

The truth was that he often
pissed me off with his "Dave Time" behavior.

I could never count on him
to do much of anything
on time.
I'd never know when he was
going to fly off to San Francisco
to have an espresso at Cafe Trieste
in North Beach just because
he liked the people
who frequented the place
like long-lost yet faithful Beatniks
or he liked the espresso that they served.

He and his wife Maria
rented a cabin in Julian
in the mountains east of San Diego
and drove the hundred miles
there and back to work
twice a week,
staying at a motel in Sunset Beach
when they were here in town.

They drove back and forth so much
that they didn't have any time left

to do their laundry so Maria had to buy
five dozen pair of panties
and two dozen bras to wear.

They got teaching jobs
on the East Coast at Chapel Hill
and took a leave of absence here
from their teaching jobs on the West Coast.

Then they took a leave of absence
at the jobs in Chapel Hill
to return to the jobs here on the West Coast.

We always wondered
just what in the hell was going on.

It seemed that they had to keep moving
or they would die like sharks.

Would it be "Dave Time" for Dave forever?

Then one night I got a call from Maria.

"You've got to come and help me.
Dave's in the hospital.
I think he's dying."

When I got there,
Maria was walking back and forth
in the hallway outside of Dave's room,
shaking her hands in front of her
like they were covered in blood
that she was trying to get off.

"I don't know.
Jesus, I don't know,
I just don't know," she said,
still shaking her hands.

Inside a doctor and nurse
were applying the paddles to Dave's chest,
making him jolt and lurch
like a wild horse over and over on the bed.

"He's had leukemia for fifteen years,
but he made me swear that I wouldn't tell anyone,"
Maria said as she walked back and forth
down the hallway while Dave
was in the bed lurching and dying,
while in Illinois the orange leaves were falling.

TEN OR ELEVEN LOST YEARS

The Indian in a feathered headdress
facing left inside a circular pattern
that looks like a target is on the TV
at our neighbor Lavonia's house,
the first TV that I have ever seen.

I lean against the chain-linked fence,
my face against the wire squares in the school-yard,
while other kids outside the fence sing
"Kindergarten baby, born in the gravy."

I am walking my new red Schwinn bicycle
along on the sidewalk in front of school,
since the bike is too tall for me to ride
and I don't even know yet how to ride a bike.

I've just gotten the bicycle license that the city
requires me to have and the license is good
until 1957 and I'm thinking that that is a long time
in the future, when I will be thirteen.

I look through the chain-linked hurricane fence
of the elementary school playground where
there are two high school guys in white t-shirts
who are in the alley fighting.

One guy is white and the other looks Japanese.
The white guy hits the Japanese guy in the face,
then the Japanese guy hits the white guy in the chest
and splits something so blood starts to squirt out of

81

the wound in the white guy's chest,
in rhythm with the white guy's heartbeat,
and the white t-shirt of the white guy turns red
from below his arms down to his new blue Levi's.

Walking through the rain in the mud in the back yard
to the smelly outhouse of my grand aunt Amelia's house
in the Colony in Santa Ana.

My father, crazy at the time and swinging a sword
that makes a humming sound above my mother's head
as my brother and I stand beside her.

The fat man from across the street
who sits on a bus bench while smoking a cigar.

As we pass with balloons on our bikes' frames
that make a rumbling sound as the spokes hit the balloon,
the fat man says, "Let me see what you have there."

Then he pops the balloon with his lit cigar.

Driving north to Camarillo mental hospital
to see my father in the blue and gray '49 Buick
with my mother and brother as I suck on lemon drops
to stop my car sickness
and watch tall eucalyptus trees slip by the car window.

A small silver flashlight that I hold then turn on,
as I watch a laughing Santa Claus at the Elk's lodge
Christmas party with Lavonia and her husband,
who have no children.

Crawling through the high grass
like a soldier in front of Mrs. Hilldale's house
as she yells from her front porch,
"You kids stay out of my grass."

The dirt that is caked and crusty behind Axel Oslund's ears,
and his skinny Okie mother who doesn't, apparently,
ever make him take a bath.

My father across the street behind the café
with a rope that has a loop on it
as he lassos a small dog with red hair
and the ears and posture of an Irish setter,
a dog that we keep and call Copper and like to yell,
"Here Copper, Copper," when a police car drives by.

The sound of the bell ringing in the flower shop
and my going from the house to the top of the stairs
and looking down at the open cash register
where a guy who looks like my half-uncle, Freddie,
is looking back up at me then running off with the money
through the front door.

The police line-up in a pea-green room where six men,
all Mexicans who look nothing like my uncle Freddie,
stand in a lineup as I look at them to pick the man I saw.

Getting punched in the right shoulder by my father
when I cannot remember six times nine equals fifty-four
as we stand in the kitchen.

Walking through the forest in the mountains
with a Belgian Police dog named Wolf.

I remember little else of my first ten or eleven years,
only vague images of teachers and family parties
and long drives into the hills and the San Bernardino mountains.

Of course, these moments happened
six or seven decades ago.
My memories of the years from the seventh grade on
would fill a telephone phone book—
which is a thick book, now extinct,
for those who have never seen one.

The good thing is that I can
make things up about those years,
and I can write about them,
whether they happened or not.

I have, in fact,
made up all of those incidents
at the beginning of this poem.

They are all fiction,
just as this statement is a fiction.

THE SQUARE

The hospital room was a trapezoid,
eight feet by ten feet by five feet by eight feet,
and Beltran couldn't stand to stay there
unless he was forced to when he was fed
through a port in his chest
for more than half an hour at a time.

When unattached from the feeding tube
that led to the vein in his chest
he walked the square path
through the hallway
of the hospital from seven a.m.
when he woke until midnight
when he took an Atavan
so that he could sleep.

This was broken only by his
being fed through his vein
the white serum.

Each day he woke up at seven
and began walking again.

He couldn't drink anything,
and he couldn't eat anything,
except when he was hooked up for hours
to the machine that fed him
through an artery.

Then another machine and tube
sucked everything that got into his stomach out,
so, the theory went,
his colon which had been sewn together
would open up and let food pass.

The nurse hooked him up to another machine
to feed him the white liquid
from a plastic bag
attached to the artery on his chest
twice a day.

He ate only Altoids,
which he wasn't even supposed to eat.

He peed but he never shit
for those two months.

The hallway where he walked made a square
through the hospital
and during the days and nights
he saw nurses and doctors
who had worked in his ward and
had been moved elsewhere,

saw visitor after visitor after visitor
who came with flowers to see friends or relatives
passing him as he walked his square
through the hallways.

When people came to visit him
he asked them to walk with him
through the square.

He never counted how many times
he walked the square in a day
yet it was at least twenty miles
because he never stopped
unless it was to be fed
through the tube in his chest.

He wasn't just going crazy,
he was crazy.

A black man who for some reason
looked to him like an African
stood behind a gray floor-cleaning machine
that moved a few inches forward each second
through the square of hallways,
day and night.

He named him
the Masai Floor Polisher.

When he shuffled past him on the square
the man moved the machine out of his path
then went back to guiding it
down the hallway,

the machine whirring softly,
moving like molten lava
through the square hallway.

For two months Beltran passed him
in the hallways
as the man guided the machine
to whirr over the floors of the hospital
day after night after day.

Beltran nodded as he passed,
and the man nodded to him,
but they said nothing to each other
day after night after day.

One night toward the end
of Beltran's stay,
when he was finally
going home to where he would also
be fed white liquid through the tube
attached in the vein in his chest,
Beltran walked the square with his wife.

When they met the Masai floor polisher
in the hallway the man looked up and said,
"He keeps me company,"
with a positively African accent.

Then he moved on
with his floor polisher
down the hallway one foot per second
as Beltran and his wife fled the clean,
white jail that is called a hospital
through the glass doors.

At home in his bed at night for weeks
he thought that he could hear
the whirr of the polishing machine
as it cleaned and moved on
through the hallways of the square.

"Forget about it," his wife said.
"It must be tinnitus."

"No, it's that African guy.
He'll be polishing that square
forever."

WHEN I HEARD THAT BUKOWSKI DIED

I was in Los Alamos, New Mexico,
and it was snowing.

I called my wife and she said,
"Did you hear that Bukowski died?"

I told her that I hadn't,
but that I knew that it was coming, sorry to say.

She said,
"Gerry called and said he was
trying to find out about the funeral."

The next morning,
I went out and got The New York Times and The L. A. Times,
the Sunday editions.

I leafed through them both
and there was not a word about Bukowski.

He'd died the Wednesday before.

I was with my brother, Rick, and I said,
"Why isn't there anything here? What do you think?"

He said, "Maybe he didn't die."

"No," I said, "Locklin told Marcia that he died."

"Yeah," Rick said, "then he died."

And I stacked the papers
and threw them in the trash,
all except the magazine section,
with the good photos of bare-breasted models
in tight jeans.

PREDATOR CONTROL

Up in the Yaak Valley, sixty miles from nowhere—
land of grizzlies, wolves, cougars, bull moose—
at Will and Claire's annual barbecue
a thirty-year-old guy in a plaid shirt
saw our foreign license plates and said,
"Up here we don't want any government
assholes telling us what to do.
We want to be left to our own devices."

His father is as deaf as El Sordo,
and I have to yell to talk to him.

He was once hired by Idaho,
in the fifties,
to do "Predator Control" in the Idaho Panhandle.

He has a black and white photograph
to prove it and he passes it around.

A dozen cougars hang dead from their necks
on a rope spread like a clothesline between two firs.

Six hatless men with suspenders hold their 30-30s
in front of them as they stand smiling at the photographer.

"Did you kill any wolves back then?" I asked.

"What?" he said. "Oh, wolves you say?
Not then, there weren't any of the bastards left.

But I'd kill every damn one of them
if they'd let me at them nowadays."

The child of the deaf man's son played
with Will's throwing tomahawk.

He threw it at the target,
which was a round,
three-foot cross-section of a fir tree,
and the tomahawk missed and clanked
to the ground over and over and over.

He just needed more practice.

The boy's stepmother, a brunette in black tights
chewing Juicy Fruit, yelled,

"Get over here and sit down!
Stop screwing around with that damn tomahawk!
Come over here and look at your grandpa's picture!
Come over here and get educated for a change!"

AN AFTERNOON WITH JACKSON POLLOCK

I.

In the Springs on Long Island
we wanted to see Jackson Pollock's grave,
if it was there.

We knew that he'd died there
in a car wreck of his own making,
so we asked a kid in a gas station:

"Do you know where Jackson Pollock's grave is?"

"Whose grave?" he said.

"Pollock. He was a painter who lived here."

"Oh," the kid said.

"How about a cemetery?"

He yelled to his friend,

"Hal, where's the cemetery around here?"

His friend was from the Springs
so he knew where the cemetery was,
just down the road.

There were a lot of trees
between the graves in the cemetery.

Pollock's gravestone was a rough,
natural gray boulder, three feet high
and shaped like an arrowhead leaning on its side.

There were a dozen pebbles on top of the stone
that people had put there for their own reasons.

In his gravestone I saw his green 1955 Oldsmobile convertible
with Pollock at the wheel,
drunk on Bourbon whiskey
and driving fast down the narrow country road
between the naked trees of fall,
a cigarette between his lips.

A blonde woman with melon-sized breasts sits beside him.
She's wearing a red sweater
and she smells of Bourbon and ten-dollar perfume.

She has her left arm across Pollock's shoulders.

Beside her riding shotgun sits a pretty brunette
in a white turtleneck.

She is drunk, but not as drunk as the other two.

She looks as if she's scared, which isn't surprising.

Pollock is thinking of the Sierra Nevadas
and the blonde hills of California
where he rode horses with his brother
and of watching the hills turn purple at twilight.

What happened to those hills? he asks himself.

II.

The three have just come from the Cedar Tavern
where De Kooning had told him,
"You're too damn drunk to drive, Jackson.
Let me take you home."

"Bullshit. I'm fine," Pollock said,
then walked right over to the fireplace
and pissed onto the flames
while the fire sizzled and stunk up the barroom.

Rothko looked over at him and shook his head,
then sipped his Scotch and thought of red paintings.

III.

Back on that country road with the two women,
the naked trees are flipping by
and Pollock thinks of his painting "Blue Poles"
as the sections of blue sky flip by.

He thinks of the old Navajo he saw
doing a sand painting on the ground,
just as he learned to do his own paintings,
and he thinks of Benton
and his pictures of the green hills of Kentucky,
then of Orozco putting Marx and Lenin
into his New York mural
to anger that rich bastard Rockefeller,

so Pollock laughs at that thought
as it starts to rain

and he comes to a turn to the left
at ninety-miles per hour
and then the Oldsmobile begins to slide then tumble,

the sky around him flashing by in green and blue
and the red of blood and the screaming women fills the air
as they tumble and tumble
with him off the road into the naked blue poles
that are only the trees that stop the 55 Olds dead as dirt.

IV.

When I snapped out of it,
my wife and I placed a black pebble on Pollock's grave
then drove off slowly and carefully
between the leafy summer trees that made a tunnel over the road.

No accidental repeats, please.

V.

At Pollock's two story house
we looked through the window
of his garage-sized studio at his black lace-up boots
that sat untied and covered with white, green, blue,
black, red and yellow paint
beside an empty sheet of plywood on the floor.

VI.

Now, years later, I remember the rough-hewn headstone,
of course,
but more than that I remember those old, black boots
covered with blobs and drips of paint.

A DESCENT INTO BAJA

He was driving his van to Enseñada,
in Baja,
to see his friend Adelberto,

and to have a few beers
and some good tequila
and some hand-made tortillas.

He'd been going to Baja for fifty years or more.

It was still one of the
"wild places" on the planet.

Miraculously.

When he was twenty or so,
before reaching the toll-road
along the coast to Enseñada

he'd often decide at midnight to take off south
even if he just had ten dollars in his pocket,
and even if he'd drunk way too much Red Mountain rotgut.

In those days
he'd put in just enough American gas in his VW
to go the hundred miles to TJ
where he could buy cheaper gas

and then drive on through TJ
and along the Peligroso road
that twisted through the inland mountains
above the valleys and the ranches
on the way to Enseñada
and then beyond for a thousand miles to Cabo.

It'd been very cheap in Mexico back then.

You only had to have enough money
for a few beers and a couple of street tacos,
a pile of corn tortillas,
a few gallons of gas and you were fine.

As he drove past Rosarita Beach
he remembered surfing at K-39
and watching a guy ride a twelve-foot swell
and then get creamed to flail away in the white water.

He wished that he still rode a board,
but that was far in the past.

Now he wouldn't eat street tacos
because he knew that he might pick up brain-eating parasites.

His brother's mother-in-law
had been diagnosed with Alzheimers
but when after a few years
she got no worse a doctor had asked her kids,

"Has she ever eaten food from the street vendors in Mexico?"

"She has a house down in Rosarita Beach," they said.

"I think that she's contracted the parasites
that many people who've eaten street tacos in Baja get."

He'd looked at them.

"No refrigeration."

At Half-Way House he remembered
stopping there for tacos and beer
just before turning to go the rest of the way
on the road that wound through the mountains.

One Christmas break his brother's art teacher
had gotten drunk on tequila
and started shooting skyrockets off a cliff
into the waves below then turned around
and slipped and fell thirty feet into the shallow water
where he'd broken his neck and died,
washing up four hours later a quarter mile down the coast.

The road to Ensenada was easy now.

All that you had to have was enough money to pay the tolls
and you drove the coastal road there in an hour or so.

He was older now and not as careless and reckless as he had been.

He didn't drink as much beer
or tequila and mescal at Hussong's Cantina,
didn't care to get stumbling drunk now,
and he also had enough money in his pockets
to buy his food in the restaurants
and cafes where they had refrigerators.

He drove past the village on the green hill
on the estuary that led to the sea,
a marina with sailboats now bobbing in the ocean breeze.

Adelberto had a store in Enseñada
that sold pots and rugs and relics of the Mata Ortiz,
the Tarahumara,
the Pima Bajo,
the Pai Pai,
the Havasupai,
the Seri,
and a few other tribes of Baja,
the Sonora and Chihuahua in Northern Mexico.

He made the turn at Sal Si Puedes
and looked down at the cove
where a good swell came around the point
like a half a dozen hands of a clock
and saw a couple of guys out
waiting for the third and best swell.

"Do it any way you can," his friend Leo had said.
"That's what Sal Si Puedes means.
The sailors on sailing ships called it that because it was
hard to catch the wind to sail out of the cove since the wind
swirled around the cove inside the cliffs."

A few ignorant Norte Americanos said,
"All Mexicans are wetbacks."

They didn't know that many people in Mexico
were still pure Indian,

that millions of the indigenous people
didn't speak Spanish at all.

Those of Mexico weren't the feather-bonneted Indians
of the cowboy movies,
but people who'd lived
as they were still living for thousands of years
and still spoke only their native language.

In Guadalajara he'd met people who were pure Spanish blood,
with blonde hair and blue eyes,
like his father's eyes.

"Ojos azules," the Indians had said,
when his father had passed away.

He'd met a red-headed Russian
whose family had been in Baja for a century.

He knew of the Chinese man
who'd changed the spelling of his name from
Hu Song to Hussong and then opened a cantina in Enseñada,

and another Chinese guy he'd encountered
had one eye and had walked up
from who-knows-where
to greet them at their camp
on a desolate beach near San Quentin.

His amigo Mike said later that he thought
that the Chinese guy had plans to kill them
and take their money,
their tent and their VW van.

Perhaps he had? But he didn't.

Now as he drove he was thirsty
and he blessed those Germans
who'd brought their formulas for fine pilsner
and lager to Guadalajara,
along with giving the mariachis
their Ump-pa-pa music for their canciones.

Ahh Bohemia, thank you.

He recalled the Japanese fisherman
who'd cast his net in the Sea of Cortez
in San Felipe and pulled out the huge Tutuava,

the Swiss innkeeper in Loreto
who'd mourned the loss of customers in his hotel
on the beach because of the evil cartels and 9/11,

Al Vela, the old gourmet from Texas
who ran a hotel on a lagoon in San Quentin
and knew Patrick Hemingway and a few astronauts
who often came and hunted the Brandt Geese
that had flown there straight from Siberia.

And so on.

Oh well.

Norte Americanos don't know a lot of things.

He recalled the young, barefoot woman
that they'd stopped to give a ride to
on a Baja dirt road in the middle of nowhere

on the sandy roads near
the coastal lagoons near San Quentin.

She looked to be seventeen at the most,
and she carried a baby wrapped in her black rebozo.

He'd asked her in Spanish where she was going,
but it was obvious from her blank expression
that she didn't understand a word he said.

What language did she speak?

He'd said simple things a few more times:

"Donde va?"

"Es este tu niño?"

But she'd looked at him as if she was deaf.

They'd driven her to the main road
where she got out and walked south
through the swirls of dust and away from town,
the baby in her arms still quiet in the black rebozo.

When he reached the cliffs
that went down to Playa Saldamando
he thought of many good times camping
with his good friends Ralph and Sally
and Jim and Suzie and Bruce and Diana
and Bill and Jan and all of their kids—
all of them in their VW vans,

their nights spent drinking tumblers
full of tequila around the fire until midnight,

barbecuing giant shrimp for dinner on the fire's coals
and then everyone eating the shrimp with their fingers.

He knew that everyone in Mexico didn't pick fruit,
mow lawns, wash dishes, or work as fry cooks
like the illegals most often did in California.

Most Norte Americanos had no idea
what Mexico was like and where its people had come from.

His friend Miguel, the architect from Mexico City, had told him,

"There's a class of Spaniards descended from the conquistadors.
 And there are other people who are descended from
the royalty of the indigenous—Aztecs, Toltecs.

"Those people are still running things.

Their ancestors never worked in the fields or built the pyramids.
That was done by the worker bees,
the peones in white shirts and guaraches.

"Those indigenous people stacked the bricks,
cooked the carne asada,
swung the hammers and did the sweating
as their ancestors have done for centuries.
So the children of Montezuma and Cortez still run the place.

"The Mojados, the wetbacks,
the people who swam the river across the border
into the states, have made everything in Mexico.

And here in the north the gringo patrons still run things,
still tell the workers and their children—
the worker bees of the hive—
what to do," Miguel had said.

So the million gallons of blood
in Zapata's and Villa's Revolution of 1910
hadn't changed the pecking order a bit.

Fifteen years back in San Javier,
an old village with only one dirt street
up the road into the mountains from Loreto on the Sea of Cortez,

he'd gone to the Fiesta de los Indios
that had been going on for a hundred and fifty years.

When he'd driven the dirt road up the mountain
he'd seen the Indian peones who were climbing
up the mountain road on their knees to do the penance
that they prayed would help them have less pain and better lives.

Around the church he saw the Indians
from across Mexico and beyond
who camped and made fires and ate their chivo
and tortillas and frijoles and drank their litros of Tecate,
their mescal or tequila while the mariachis played their canciones.

Once he and his friends had ridden mules
into the Canyon of Guadalupe in the mountains
of central Baja and he'd seen the pictographs of giants
with antennae and breaching whales and mountain goats
and abstract patterns,

those paintings of figures who were perhaps constellations
were said to be three thousand,
or maybe ten thousand,
years old,
painted by the ancient ancestors of the current residents.

Another time in Bahia de Los Angeles
he and his friend Ben had gone to a small circus
right out of *La Strada*,
the tent above them sending a fog of mist
down on the spectators and performers
from the pelting rainstorm outside.

Now he wondered if his 12.5 % of native blood
connected him somehow to these people
and this wild land of Baja and beyond.

He thought of the five-foot-two Zapotec
farm workers drinking liters of Tecate
and the transvestite bartenders in the bar in San Quentin
whom he saw with his friend John,

and then the night that they stood and watched
the starlight frame the volcanos
and the stars reflecting their distant light on the lagoon.

At the final toll-booth of the highway
along the cliffs he looked to see if there were any waves
breaking at San Miguel,
then he drove past the shipyard into town.

First he went to Hussong's Cantina
and ordered a shot of Herradura
and a Pacifico as he stood there

in that two hundred year old cantina
and listened to the mariachis play a song
by Santana, which was a surprise.

Soon he would go to see his friend Alberto
and talk and have coffee and a tequila
and perhaps buy a Mata Ortiz pot
or one of his paintings to take home
even though he had dozens of pots and paintings
and relics at home.

It was two in the afternoon
and there were only a few people in the bar
and there weren't as many gringos
as there had been in the past
because of the rumors of deaths and decapitations.

But it was a good cantina still.

It looked just as it had years ago
except for a few new mariachis
and a couple of new bartenders
who'd only been working there
twenty and thirty years.

No, he thought.
It isn't like the old days.

But so what?

Like the old guy in the movie said,
"It'll do."

THE LAST GOOD BEACH

The sign on the walkway to the beach said: NO CAMPING, NO ALCOHOL, NO BOTTLES, NO SMOKING, NO SAILBOARD-ING, and of course NO DOGS, yet Beltran took his dog through the private gate whose combination a friend had given him, then down the way a hundred yards that hadn't been walled off yet, then out past one more sign that said NO DOGS. He was just out of sight from a lifeguard who'd been hired to watch and save people on his side of the fence, and to make sure that everyone followed the NO-EVERYTHING rules that someone in Hell or Congress or City Hall had decided were needed for peace, safety and tranquility on the beaches of the city in the County of the Damned and Idiot-ic. A year earlier, he had been on that same beach and had watched from down the shoreline as a Rent-a-Cop of some kind—his Glock in his holster—had pounced upon an old lady with blue hair who had brought her Border Collie out on the beach to run and fetch a chartreuse tennis ball. Beltran watched from 150 yards as the Rent-a-Cop stood talking and shaking his finger at the old woman, her head down in disgrace. The Rent-a-Cop left and went back through the break in the side-by-side houses and the old woman walked down the beach as if she was going toward home until the Rent-a-Cop was out of sight and back inside the beach colony of the Nouveau Rich, a place that a friend who lived there called My Phony Malibu, their three-story houses standing like open refrigerators a hundred feet from the surf-line and down the way from the Federal Ammo Depot. When she saw that the Rent-a-Cop was gone she turned and walked back to the water's edge and threw the chartreuse tennis ball and played with her Border Collie as if the Rent-a-Cop had never spoken to her. Then when Beltran had come next to her with his dog beside him, the woman had said, "We've got to do something about this bloody country. It's a goddamned police state lately." And he said,

"That it is, ma'am, but what can we do except break their stupid laws?" She said, "We can vote them out and impeach the dog Nazis. We can write letters to the Times." Then he said, "That's a plan." So she said, "We can do it together." "Maybe we can," he said. She shrugged and he shrugged and she walked north and he south in their separate directions down the beach, both of them throwing their tennis balls over and over into the water and down the way below the surf-line. He had been breaking the law and coming to this beach with his various dogs for more than four decades, only getting caught by a woman-dog-catcher and anti-dog-zealot, who gave him a ticket for having his dog on the beach without a leash and who said, "Never bring your dog out here again, or you will really be in big trouble, sir." Not saying what "big trouble" was. So the fine was one hundred and fifty dollars and he'd divided that amount by forty-odd years and come up with a number, then divided that number by three-hundred and sixty-five and come up with 0.01027397 cents a day, an amount that he figured was a fair charge for bringing his dog to the beach where he loved to walk and watch his dog run at full speed to get the ball even before he threw it, then stop by some dog radar at exactly the distance that he had thrown it, then watch the golden retriever go down on her belly in the thin layer of water of the shore-break and cool herself down with dog air-conditioning. Now he walked with his dog, his fourth dog that he'd brought here to the Last Good Beach in the county. He faithfully carried a blue plastic bag to pick up the dog-shit, not relishing the thought of him or anyone else stepping in the stuff and having it squish up between his toes or of any of his kids' or someone else's kids using the fresh turds for parapets on their sand castles. He threw the tennis ball as far as he could and the Golden Retriever darted after it and caught it on the first bounce, then pranced around with the prize in her mouth and finally dropped it onto the packed dark sand and rolled on it as well as some nearby seaweed that she fancied, trying to mark it with her scent, no doubt, and trying to smell like as much stinky stuff as she could as well.

Now, at seven p.m., it was usually safe to come to the Last Good Beach, since the lifeguard was long-gone, yet Beltran knew that one of these days the woman-dogcatcher-zealot, or some similar jerk, would come driving a four-wheel-drive pickup down the beach and hand him another ticket, which he would pay, perhaps, by sending first $1.50, instead of $150, and they would write him saying "No, not $1.50, it's $150, so you now owe $148.50." So he would send them $14.85, and he would continue being nuts in that manner, hoping that they would think him so stupid that they would give up the chase. Whatever happened, he would enjoy driving them nuts a few times. And of course he would continue to bring his current Golden Retriever and even his next Golden Retriever to the Last Good Beach in the county whether they liked it or not. Happily, there was currently a recession, so they couldn't afford as many woman-zealot-dogcatchers and lifeguards as they needed to scour the beaches and keep it safe and clear of anyone with the audacity to bring their dog there. Thank the gods, he thought, for recessions and bad financial times. I'haven't seen a zealot for a while. At least bad times are good for something.

AUTHOR BIO

RAFAEL ZEPEDA is a Professor of English at California State University, Long Beach. His previous books include *Horse Medicine & Other Stories, Tao Driver and Selected Poems, The Wichita Poems, The Yellow Ford of Texas, The Durango Poems,* and *Desperados.* His poems and stories have appeared in many anthologies and magazines. He has received a National Endowment of the Arts Creative Writing Fellowship in Fiction, a California Artists' Fellowship, and a Poets, Essayists and Novelists Syndicated Fiction Award.

CPSIA information can be obtained
at www.ICGtesting.com
Printed in the USA
FSHW020155170820

9 781733 784818